Date: 1/19/16

BR 381.41 LIN
Lindeen, Mary,
A visit to the market /

PALM BEACH COUNTY
LIBRARY SYSTEM
3650 SUMMIT BLVD.
WEST PALM BEACH, FL 33406

A Beginning-to-Read Book

A Visit to the Market

by Mary Lindeen

NORWOOD HOUSE PRESS

DEAR CAREGIVER, The *Beginning to Read—Read and Discover* books provide emergent readers the opportunity to explore the world through nonfiction while building early reading skills. The text integrates both common sight words and content vocabulary. These key words are featured on lists provided at the back of the book to help your child expand his or her sight word recognition, which helps build reading fluency. The content words expand vocabulary and support comprehension.

Nonfiction text is any text that is factual. The Common Core State Standards call for an increase in the amount of informational text reading among students. The Standards aim to promote college and career readiness among students. Preparation for college and career endeavors requires proficiency in reading complex informational texts in a variety of content areas. You can help your child build a foundation by introducing nonfiction early. To further support the CCSS, you will find Reading Reinforcement activities at the back of the book that are aligned to these Standards.

Above all, the most important part of the reading experience is to have fun and enjoy it!

Sincerely,

Shannon Cannon, Ph.D.
Literacy Consultant

Norwood House Press • P.O. Box 316598 • Chicago, Illinois 60631
For more information about Norwood House Press please visit our website at www.norwoodhousepress.com or call 866-565-2900.
© 2016 Norwood House Press. Beginning-to-Read™ is a trademark of Norwood House Press. All rights reserved. No part of this book may be reproduced or utilized in any form or by any means without written permission from the publisher.

Editor: Judy Kentor Schmauss
Designer: Lindaanne Donohoe

Photo Credits:
Shutterstock, cover, 1, 4-5, 6, 8-9, 10-11, 12-13, 14-15, 16, 17, 18-19, 20-21, 22, 23, 24-25; Dreamstime, 3 (©Goran Bogicevic), 26-27 and 28-29 (MangoStock); Phil Martin, 7

Library of Congress Cataloging-in-Publication Data
    Lindeen, Mary, author.
     A visit to the market / by Mary Lindeen.
       pages cm. – (A beginning to read book)
     Summary: "Take a trip to a farmer's market. You can buy fruits, vegetables, flowers, and other homemade products there. See how the farmers sell their produce. This title includes reading activities and a word list"– Provided by publisher.
     Audience: K to grade 3
     ISBN 978-1-59953-692-7 (library edition : alk. paper)
     ISBN 978-1-60357-777-9 (ebook)
     1. Farmers' markets–Juvenile literature. 2. Family farms–Juvenile literature.
     3. Farm produce–Juvenile literature. I. Title.
     HF5470.L56 2015
     381.41-dc23
                                                       2014047632

Manufactured in the United States of America in Stevens Point, Wisconsin. 275N-062015

Look at all of these people.
Where do you think they are going?

They are going to the market!

Farmers grow food and flowers.

Then they sell the food and flowers at the market.

Would you like some beans?

Here they are!

Would you like some carrots?

Here they are!

Would you like some apples?

Here they are!

Would you like some pumpkins?

Here they are!

Would you like some jam?

It was made from strawberries.

You can taste some honey.

Would you like to buy some?

Look at all of these fruits and vegetables.

Which would you like to buy?

Look at all of these flowers.

What colors do you see?

Did you get everything you wanted?

Put it all in the car.

It is time to go home.

The market is going to close.

This farmer is getting ready to go home.

He will be back another day.

See you at the market!

...READING REINFORCEMENT...

CRAFT AND STRUCTURE

To check your child's understanding of this book, recreate the following diagram on a sheet of paper. Read the book with your child, and then help him or her fill in the diagram using what they learned. Work together to complete the diagram by writing the main idea of the book and several details relating to it:

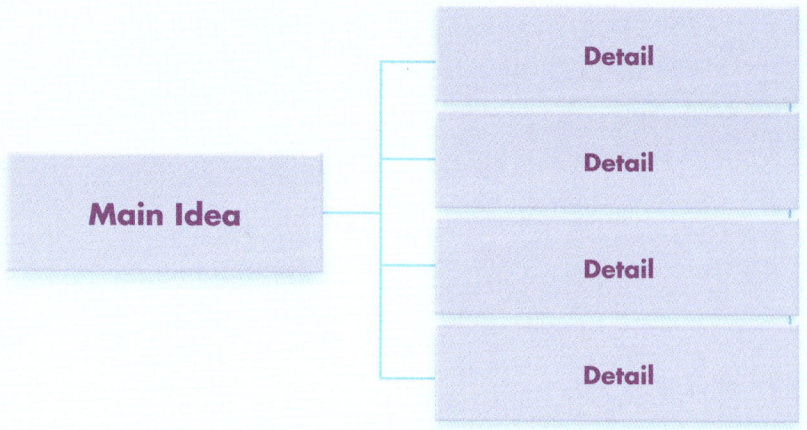

VOCABULARY: Learning Content Words

Content words are words that are specific to a particular topic. All of the content words for this book can be found on page 32. Use some or all of these content words to complete one or more of the following activities:

- Help your child make up riddles for which content words are the answers.
- Have your child identify a content word by using three clues you provide; for example, *green, lima, pinto* ➔ *beans*.
- Have your child choose a content word and draw a picture to illustrate its meaning.
- Help your child find pairs of content words that have something in common, either in meaning, structure, or both.
- Write the content words on slips of paper. Place them in a box. Have your child pick a word and use it in a sentence.

FOUNDATIONAL SKILLS: *r*-controlled vowels

When a vowel (*a, e, i, o, u*) comes before the letter *r*, the sound of the vowel changes. This is called an *r*-controlled vowel. Have your child identify the *r*-controlled vowels in the words below. Then ask your child to find words with *r*-controlled vowels in this book.

| market | are | flowers | colors |
| farmer | car | another | everything |

CLOSE READING OF INFORMATIONAL TEXT

Close reading helps children comprehend text. It includes reading a text, discussing it with others, and answering questions about it. Use these questions to discuss this book with your child:

- What is a farmer's market?
- What can you buy at a farmer's market?
- What might happen if it rained at a farmer's market?
- Why might farmers sell their produce at a farmer's market?
- How could you find out if there is a farmer's market near you?
- What would you like to sell at a farmer's market if you could?

FLUENCY

Fluency is the ability to read accurately with speed and expression. Help your child practice fluency by using one or more of the following activities:

- Reread this book to your child at least two times while he or she uses a finger to track each word as you read it.
- Read the first sentence aloud. Then have your child reread the sentence with you. Continue until you have finished this book.
- Ask your child to read aloud the words they know on each page of this book. (Your child will learn additional words with subsequent readings.)
- Have your child practice reading this book several times to improve accuracy, rate, and expression.

••• Word List •••

A Visit to the Market uses the 66 words listed below. *High-frequency* words are those words that are used most often in the English language. They are sometimes referred to as sight words because children need to learn to recognize them automatically when they read. *Content words* are any words specific to a particular topic. Regular practice reading these words will enhance your child's ability to read with greater fluency and comprehension.

High-Frequency Words

all	did	is	some	want(ed)
and	do	it	the	was
another	from	like	then	what
are	get(ing)	look	these	where
at	go(ing)	made	they	which
back	he	of	think	will
be	here	people	this	would
can	home	put	time	you
day	in	see	to	

Content Words

apples	close	food	market	taste
beans	colors	fruits	pumpkins	vegetable
buy	everything	grow	ready	
car	farmer(s)	honey	sell	
carrots	flowers	jam	strawberries	

••• About the Author

Mary Lindeen is a writer, editor, parent, and former elementary school teacher. She has written more than 100 books for children and edited many more. She specializes in early literacy instruction and books for young readers, especially nonfiction.

••• About the Advisor

Dr. Shannon Cannon is a teacher educator in the School of Education at UC Davis, where she also earned her Ph.D. in Language, Literacy, and Culture. She serves on the clinical faculty, supervising pre-service teachers and teaching elementary methods courses in reading, effective teaching, and teacher action research.